EARTH

AS A WEAPON OF
DEFENCE OR WARFARE

Pastor Uzor Ndekwu

EARTH
AS A WEAPON OF
DEFENCE OR WARFARE

Pastor Uzor Ndekwu

Edited by Chris Newton

MEMOIRS
Cirencester

United Kingdom:

Uzor Ndekwu Ministries (Jesus Sanctuary)
25/27 Ruby Street
Old Kent Road
London SE15 1LR
United Kingdom
Tel: +44 207 277 5664; +44 7961 276 187
Email: info@jesussanctuaryministries.org
Website: www.jesussanctuaryministries.org

Nigeria:

Uzor Ndekwu Ministries (Jesus Sanctuary)
41 Otigba Crescent
GRA
Onitsha
Anambra State
Nigeria
Te: +234 803 395 0197; +234 803 405 2113

Published by:

Uzor Ndekwu Ministries (Jesus Sanctuary)

Bible quotations are from the King James Version of the Holy Bible.

Printed in England by: Memoirs Publishers

ISBN 978-1-908223-36-4

EARTH
AS A WEAPON OF
DEFENCE OR WARFARE

TABLE OF CONTENTS: **Page**

ACKNOWLEDGEMENTS

I wish to express my profound thanks to the following persons: my wife for her help and support and for checking and editing the original draft, Pastor Obi (Pastor of Jesus Sanctuary Ministries, Onitsha Branch) for the insightful testimonies, Dr. Osakwe Chinweuba (the former occultist who gave his life to Christ and is now a Minister of God) for his powerful insights into the activities of occultic people using the Earth, Brother Andrew Onwuemene who typed the original manuscript and to Mr. Chris Newton for the editing and proof-reading of the book.

CHAPTER ONE

BACKGROUND

I am a member of the Ibo tribe/people of Nigeria, and I spent most of my early years in the village – Ubulu-Uku, in Delta State. I was always fascinated by the way the elders of our tribe regarded the Earth. For them, it is a living entity which is animate, active and responsive. They believe the Earth can see, hear, speak, eat and even adjudicate in family and communal matters.

This bond of relationship between them and the Earth is all encompassing, and has all the characteristics of a covenant. The bond is exemplified in numerous ways but can be illustrated by six traditional customs:

1. BREAKING OF KOLA NUTS

During formal or informal gatherings, the elders used kola nuts, the fruit of the kola tree, to make demands and ask for assistance from the Earth. A piece of the nut is placed on the Earth and the remaining pieces are shared among those present.

2. MEAL OR FOOD SACRIFICE

When food is cooked the Earth is offered a portion and the remainder is divided among those present. As a child, I enjoyed this aspect of sacrifice because it meant there was always enough to eat.

3. LIBATION OFFERING

This is known as drink offering. The elders speak into the cup of drink and pour a quantity on the Earth, while the rest is shared out among those present.

4. BLOOD SACRIFICE

This is basically for atonement and appeasement. Part of the blood is poured on to the Earth, while the carcase of the animal is shared among the participants.

5. PERIOD OF REVERENCE

Every year, some days are earmarked to revere the Earth. No economic work is carried out in such days.

6. CELEBRATORY OFFERING

Every year, there are days when the community sing, dance and worship the Earth.

These practices demonstrate the value the elders place on the Earth as a formidable and vital ally in their existence and well-being. The traditional belief of my people is that you cannot derive Earth's full benefits until you understand its secrets. For them, the strength of the bond between them and the Earth is based on the fact that God made us from the Earth; and it is to the Earth, we shall return, when we die. So, the Earth is the womb of the living and the dead. One can therefore appreciate and understand why my people place much value on their relationship with the Earth. Their inestimable spiritual and physical value of the Earth is based on the fact that they depend on it for their growth, multiplication, survival and preservation. No wonder land issues are matters of life and death. So many families, communities, kindreds and even nation-states have lost many lives as a result of bitter and acrimonious contentions over land.

It is interesting to note also that there is a spiritual angle when it comes to land contention or adjudication issues. On a general note, one can safely say that victory over land matters does not depend only on the 'rightful' owner, but on who has more 'spiritual connection' with the gods of the land. And the spiritual connection is based on who has "sacrificed" and spoken to the Earth more authoritatively. That is why most land disputes in court do not end conclusively because the vulnerable party usually withdraws from pursuing justice or dies suddenly.

When I became an adult and my relationship with God grew deeper through studying the Bible, I realised that my people's understanding of the Earth's nature resonates with the biblical narratives. From Genesis to Revelations, God and His ministers (servants) treated the Earth as a living entity. During and after creation, God spoke with the Earth as if it was a living entity; and the Earth responded accordingly to God's commands. When the Earth was without form and void and covered in darkness, it was the spoken word of God that brought order to the otherwise shapeless, empty and formless Earth. The scripture says:

> *"In the beginning God created the heaven and the Earth. And the Earth was without form, and void; and darkness was upon the face of the deep... And God said, Let there be light: and there was light... And God said, Let the Earth bring forth the living creature after his kind, cattle, and creeping thing, and beast"* (Genesis 1:1-24).

As you can see, God was communicating with the Earth by giving commands and the Earth was responding to the instructions accordingly. God's words made the Earth release her resources by bringing forth the living and non-living creatures in her womb.

The personal lesson here is that no matter how formless, empty, lifeless, unproductive, useless or hopeless your situation or condition appears, once you allow the light of God to shine upon you through His Son and the studying of the words of God, your circumstances will turn around for good. You can be in a position to change what is wrong in your family, your business or any part of your life.

CHAPTER TWO

THE EARTH AND MAN

God equally related to the Earth as an entity from another dimension when it came to the creation of man. He did not command us to come forth. Instead, He sowed a prophetic seed of His breath into the Earth. This He did when a mist from the Earth watered the ground. He formed and moulded man after His likeness and image, breathed into the nostrils of the shaped image the breath of life, and man became a living soul. According to the Bible:

> *"But there went up a mist from the earth, and watered the whole face of the ground... And the LORD God formed man of the dust of the ground, and breathed into his nostrils the breath of life; and man became a living soul."*
> Genesis 2:6-7.

From the above verses of the scripture, it is clear that man was deliberately and purposely created by God. Man was not an accident of the environment. Therefore the issue of evolution of man is simply a scientific fiction. We were made after the image and likeness of God, and each of us has our individuality that originated from God. That is why no two persons, even identical twins, have the same DNA.

Another area God related with the Earth is when it comes to the issue of blessings. According to the scripture, God entered into a covenant with the Earth, and placed man in charge of the Earth realm.

In Genesis 9:13, God said:

> *"I do set my bow in the cloud, and it shall be for a token of a covenant between me and the earth."*

And in Psalm 115:16, the scripture says:

> *"The heaven, even the heavens, are the LORD's: but the earth hath he given to the children of men."*

THE EARTH AND SIN:

When Adam and Eve sinned, two things happened to the Earth. First, Adam and Eve lost their authority and dominion of the Earth to satan, and Satan became the prince of this Earth. That is why, at the first meeting between Jesus and satan, he (satan) offered Jesus Christ the glory and kingdoms of this world, if He (Jesus) will worship him, which Jesus flatly rejected. This episode shows that before Jesus conquered satan at Calvary, satan was indeed the prince of the world. This encounter is recorded in Matthew 4:8-10:

> *"Again, the devil taketh him up into an exceeding high mountain, and sheweth him all the kingdoms of the world, and the glory of them; And saith unto him, All these things will I give thee, if thou wilt fall down and worship me. Then saith Jesus unto him, Get thee hence, Satan: for it is written, Thou shalt worship the Lord thy God, and him only shalt thou serve."*

The second thing that happened when Adam and Eve sinned was that the Earth was cursed by God. As recorded in Genesis 3:17, God said:

".........Because thou hast hearkened unto the voice of thy wife, and hast eaten of the tree, of which I commanded thee, saying, Thou shalt not eat of it: cursed is the ground for thy sake; in sorrow shalt thou eat of it all the days of thy life".

So the Earth which God originally said was good (Genesis 1:10) after creation, was cursed by Him as well because of man's sin. Thus the Earth became an instrument of blessing or cursing. As a consequence of this, the attributes of responding to commands, hearing and speaking that the Earth acquired as a result of God's relationship with the Earth became also channels through which evil can be perpetrated. As will be seen in subsequent paragraphs, people can therefore use the Earth for wicked purposes by speaking or commanding the Earth to work against the destiny of people.

Conversely, the Earth can be used to bless

people during marriages and other festive periods as we earlier mentioned in most traditional communities. On balance, those who have the spiritual understanding of the Earth can use it either as an instrument of blessing or cursing.

THE EARTH AND MEN OF GOD:

All through the scriptures, men of God used the Earth as an instrument of warfare or blessing. Moses used it as an instrument of warfare in Egypt, causing plagues of lice.

> *"And the LORD said unto Moses, Say unto Aaron, stretch out thy rod, and smite the dust of the land, that it may become lice throughout all the land of Egypt... Aaron stretched out his hand with his rod, and smote the dust of the Earth, and it became lice in man, and in beast; all the dust of the land became lice throughout all the land of Egypt."*
> *Exodus 8:16-17.*

In another instance, as Moses was speaking, the Earth responded by opening her mouth to swallow those provoking him:

> *"And the Earth opened her mouth, and swallowed them up, and their houses, and all the men"* (Numbers 16:31-32).

Almost all the servants of God in the scriptures utilised the services of the Earth. Prophet Isaiah said:

> *"Hear, O heavens, and give ear, O Earth…"* (Isaiah 1:2).

Prophet Micah decreed:

> *"Hear, all ye people; hearken, O Earth, and all …." (Micah 1:2).*

For Prophet Jeremiah:

> *"O Earth, Earth, Earth, hear the word of the LORD. Thus saith the LORD, Write ye this man childless, a man that shall not prosper in his days: for no man of his seed shall prosper, sitting upon the throne of David."* (Jeremiah 22:29-30).

The king that Jeremiah cursed with the Earth who is known as Jehoiachin (Coniah), never had a son, and when he eventually adopted seven sons of Neri *(1 Chronicles 3:15-20)*, none of the boys nor their children mounted the throne of David. The closest a grandson of King Jehoiachin achieved was to become a governor *(Ezra 2:2)*.

Even Jesus Christ advised us to use the dust of the Earth as a witness against those that refuse the good news.

> *"And whosoever shall not receive you, nor hear your words, when ye depart out of that house or city, shake off the dust of your feet (Matthew 10:14)*;

and in healing a blind man.

> *"When he had thus spoken, he spat on the ground, and made clay of the spittle, and he anointed the eyes of the blind man with the clay, And said unto him, Go, wash in the pool of Siloam..., and washed, and came seeing" (John 9:6-7)*.

The story of Prophet Jeremiah and King Jehoiachin (Coniah) is a good example of how the Earth can be used to derail, stop, frustrate, delay, and destroy the destiny of a person or generation of people *(Jeremiah 22:29-30; 1 Chronicles 3:15-20)*. In our time, wicked ones still employ the Earth's services to fight, derail or stop the future of their ignorant victims. Scripture says that

> *"My people are destroyed for lack of knowledge: because thou hast rejected knowledge, I will also reject thee..."* *(Hosea 4:6)*.

And Jesus Christ said:

> *"...for the children of this world are in their generation wiser than the children of light."* *(Luke 16:8)*.

The stories of some victims who suffered as a result of their oppressors, the confessions of a native doctor and an occult grandmaster that turned to become servants of God, show clearly that the Earth can be used to control the destinies of ignorant people, as the following cases show:

CHAPTER THREE

CASE STUDIES

CASE 1: Mrs. Stone

Mrs. Stone was childless for more than seven years. The problem was basically her mother-in-law, who had never wanted her son to marry her. All attempts to discourage the son failed. The reason for her refusal to give consent to the marital union was that she was an "Osu" (outcast) in their village and moreover, her family did not share the same faith (Mrs Stone's family were Catholics and the girl's people were Anglicans). When their son resisted and eventually married the girl in a Pentecostal church, the parents of the boy decided to frustrate the marriage. The boy's uncle was a native doctor, who was implored to help them frustrate this couple. In course of time, Mrs. Stone's husband helped by giving the uncle's son a job in the banking industry. As a result, the uncle confessed to the couple that he was raising the Earth of their family compound to the new moon every month to speak against their conception. That coincided with the bleeding experiences Mrs Stone normally experienced every time she became pregnant. She eventually reversed the curse and became a mother (2003).

CASE 2: MR JAMES C

James C came from a polygamous family, where the father had three wives. He was the first son of the third wife. Among his siblings, James was well-to-do and the star of the family. However, the first wife, his father's senior wife, decided out of jealousy to hire a native doctor to help transfer the good fortunes of James to her own first son, who was not doing so well and was struggling with his business. The native doctor raised an altar of Earth and used James' footprints to place a curse to ensure that as long as he walked on the face of the Earth, the Earth would afflict him. This promising young man's business and health began to dwindle until he died. The next son then began to suffer the same ailment and affliction. If it had not been for the deliverance sessions and prayers said on their landed properties, James' brother could not have survived, but he is now a Minister of God in Nigeria. Cases of brothers and sisters with the same marital, mental and infirmity issues or undue delays and frustrations over the years are traceable most times to an invocation of the curse covenant upon the Earth. And those who do not exercise authority or know their God are usually frustrated, spiritually marginalised, hopeless, helpless and even, at times, destroyed.

CHAPTER FOUR

THE EARTH AFFLICTIONS

We have handled cases where the wicked ones deposit or bury charms in the compounds of their victims. The charms attract a negative aura that slows down the building or project development. Cases of uncompleted buildings are traceable to spiritual manipulation of the owners. In some instances, the income that is financing the project dries up; some die before completion or lose their jobs, or their businesses suffer heavy losses. The need to dedicate your business or building projects to God cannot be over-emphasised. Even traditional building projects are subjected to some rituals. As children of God, men of God should always dedicate the foundation of their projects.

In other cases the wicked ones sacrifice and mix the blood of animals, blood of fowls of the air and/or the blood of 'creeping things' with the Earth. Satanic divination and enchantment empowers the mixture which demonises the

Earth. The blood content of that Earth is a force of demonic attraction and visitation. When it is thrown into their victim's compound or property, all sorts of strange movements and sounds are noticed in the affected area. If not checked through intercessory prayer and deliverance, the compounds are usually abandoned, opening the way to house demons and becoming a haunted place.

At times the wicked ones create a pit or an open grave, and the victim's names, pictures, effigy, are thrown into it and by means of enchantment and divinations, the victim's names are intermittently invoked, with the hope that the victim will suddenly die. Most people who see themselves in dreams around pits, graveyards, and valleys are being manipulated spiritually for untimely burial. King Solomon said:

> *"Whoso diggeth a pit shall fall therein...*
> *" (Proverbs 26:27).*

Before I became a pastor, a rich friend of mine

whom I saw in a deep valley in a dream became not only poor but so wretched that he could not take care of his family. In 2006, I saw him in London working illegally as a cleaner. He was a shadow of his old self. When you see yourself in such a dream, the need to embark on fasting and prayers to cancel the enchantment and divination of the enemies cannot be over-emphasized. The scripture says:

> *"Surely there is no enchantment against Jacob, neither is there any divination against Israel: according to this time it shall be said of Jacob and of Israel, What hath God wrought!"* (Numbers 23:23).

The following examples from a former native doctor and occult grandmaster who is now a child of God will help back this up:

1. When men want to do evil, they gather some Earth from a new grave site. Then they obtain a dead snake that was killed on the road by a vehicle. They will then invoke the spirit of the victim into the snake and drop it on a highway. If the would-be victim is not a child of God, any time a vehicle crushes that dead snake, the victim will die.

2. Another method, which is the commonest among the Ibos, is termed 'using of foot or car tyre prints'. This according to him, is a simple method. The evil people collect the sand and after the usual ritual, they bury it in the grave where someone who died by accident was buried.

3. According to him, the most secret and rare method among the élite class all over the world is referred to as the 'full of harpies' method. This is because most of the practitioners are women. Their method of application is to make sure that they collect some sand from the would-be victim's ancestral home or compound. They also collect left-over crumbs of food eaten by the person. After all the verbal spells, they will mix it with any food or meat which they know that the animal or bird they choose to use will eat. Once that animal or bird eats it, the job is well done. The consequences are terrible, eg death and all forms of mental disorder.

In summary, from experiences during counselling sessions, the underlisted occurrences may be the direct outcome of satanic pronouncements to the Earth by the wicked ones upon their victims:

1. CHILDLESSNESS
There are numerous instances of wicked people using the Earth to stop others from having children.

2. MISCARRIAGE/THREATENED ABORTION
Some miscarriages are facilitated by blood-sucking demons of the land that have been contracted through raising satanic altars of the Earth. Constant and periodic attacks are made at a particular month or season.

3. CONSTANT MENSTRUAL FLOW
Most women who suffer this are easily delivered once they are anointed to stop the blood-sucking demons.

4. SICKNESS OR DISEASES
We have counselled and prayed for some family members whose affliction runs through their bloodline. The Earth is usually used to afflict

victims. In 2005, four members of the same family died of strokes within a 10-month period. In London in January 2011, a woman reported that her father, mother, elder brother and sisters had all died within seven months.

5. TERMINAL DISEASES

There are families where cancer was diagnosed as the cause of death and a member dies every year. It was family deliverance that stopped the mouth of the lions.

6. ACCIDENTS

When members of the same family begin to die of road accidents, the general trend is that the power of the Earth (grave) has been activated against the family. In my town, Ubulu-Uku in Delta State, Nigeria, three family members were killed by road accidents.

7. SUICIDAL TENDENCIES

These have been associated with unrighteous decrees invoked through afflicting victims with the spirit of death by engaging the demons of the land or Earth.

8. UNCOMPLETED PROJECTS
Satanic and demonic charms are usually buried or thrown into the would-be victim's compound or premises and the source of finance for that project is attacked.

9. NEAR-SUCCESS SYNDROME
Failure or frustration at the point of success is an Earth bound projection to reverse the destiny of the victim.

10. MORBIDITY
Constant fear and anxiety are projected when the victim's name is enchanted by asking the demons of the Earth to keep tormenting the mind-set of their victim.

11. SPIRITUAL UNPRODUCTIVITY
One of the ways the wicked ones fight the children of God is to arrest their prayer life spiritually. The charmed dust of the Earth is usually placed at the gate, door, or entrance of their would-be victim. Once the person steps into their home or office, the desire and willingness to pray or study the bible is gone. Instead, they will start listening to carnal news. From the foregoing, the fact that the Earth can

be used as an instrument of blessing or cursing is not in doubt. My concern is that most people, who are children of God, do not know how to exercise their redemptive rights in the Name and Blood of Jesus Christ, by commanding the Earth to work for them.

Scriptures made us understand that before the death of Jesus Christ at Calvary, the Earth was under the effective rulership of Satan and his cohorts. That is why Satan offered Jesus Christ the kingdom of the Earth on their first contact.

"Again, the devil taketh him up into an exceeding high mountain, and sheweth him all the kingdoms of the world, and the glory of them; And saith unto him, All these things will I give thee, if thou wilt fall down and worship me." (Matthew 4:8-9).

At Calvary, what Jesus rejected during temptation season became ours immediately the Blood of Jesus touched the Earth and Satan lost dominion over the Earth. As it quaked, the graves were opened and the bodies of the saints who slept arose.

"Jesus, when he had cried again with a loud voice, yielded up the ghost. And, behold, the veil of the temple was rent in twain from the top to the bottom; and the Earth did quake, and the rocks rent; And the graves were opened; and many bodies of the saints which slept arose" *(Matthew 27:50-53).*

What man lost through Adam was regained by our Lord Jesus Christ.

As redeemed children of God, we now have the power and authority to access and enter into the Earth's fullness. For we are made to exercise dominion and profit from the Earth. Everything that has contact with the Earth is dependent on it for its growth, nurturing, survival and rest. That is why we say "Mother Earth". What a good mother is to the children is what the Earth ought to be to us.

Given this understanding, you can now command the Earth to hear you. Then you can exercise dominion over it and reverse situations and circumstances that are contrary to God's will and ordination for your life. God used the spoken word to bring light upon the Earth, that was formless and void. And the Earth thereafter began to manifest its resourcefulness. The words that you speak or decree can change your situation if aligned with the words of God. Job said:

"Thou shalt also decree a thing, and it shall be established unto thee: and the light shall shine upon thy ways." (Job 22:28).

So you can live in dominion and arrest the four things that King Solomon said make the Earth to be disquieted.

"For three things the Earth is disquieted, and for four which it cannot bear: For a servant when he reigneth; and a fool when he is filled with meat; For an odious woman when she is married; and an handmaid that is heir to her mistress." (Proverbs 30:21-23).

What King Solomon is saying is that many people are far from achieving the purpose of God for their lives. The need to use God's words and command the Earth about your today, tomorrow, future, family, children, friends, enemies and businesses cannot be overstated. It is vital that you rule your world through decrees, because, that is the language of the spiritual world. You can instruct or direct the Earth to release your blessings and not to understand the voice or voices of the wicked ones. As Prophet Isaiah said:

"Woe unto them that decree unrighteous decrees, and that write grievousness which they have prescribed" (Isaiah 10:1).

You can command the Earth to obey your voice as God, Moses, Isaiah, Jeremiah, Micah, and Jesus did.

So in the next chapter, there are two sections. Firstly, there are series of prayer points that are derived from the words of God, which can be used to cancel unrighteous decrees, ordinances, proclamations, divinations and/or enchantments. Scriptures says the word of God is the Sword of the Spirit:

"… and the sword of the Spirit, which is the word of God" (Ephesians 6:17).

The second deals with the prophetic: you use the words of God to exercise your dominion on Earth as ordained by God.

> *"And God said, Let us make man in our image, after our likeness: and let them have dominion over the fish of the sea, and over the fowl of the air, and over the cattle, and over all the Earth, and over every creeping thing that creepeth upon the Earth."* (Genesis 1:26).

Are you ready to dominate the Earth? For God told Jeremiah:

> *"I have made the Earth, the man and the beast that are upon the ground, by my great power and by my outstretched arm, and have given it unto whom it seemed meet unto me." (Jeremiah 27:5).*

> *And King David reminded us that... but the Earth hath he given to the children of men." (Psalms 115:16).*

Why not command the Earth to yield to you her increase?

CHAPTER FIVE

TESTIMONIES

I know the following testimonies will bless you. Firstly, they show how some people prayed using the Earth, and secondly, what they achieved after praying with the Earth.

■ Sister Jennifer's husband packed out of their home and started living with a neighbour more than twice her age. Despite serious prayers, her husband refused to come back. During one of the church programs, the theme involved everyone praying with the Earth. She however, did not stop there. She took the Earth home and continued praying with it for seven days, using it as a point of contact to separate her husband from the woman. After the seven days, she threw the earth away. Less than one week after, her husband quarrelled with the lady and packed back into their matrimonial home.

■ Sister Augustina was barren for twenty-one years. After hearing the teaching on using the Earth to pray, her eyes opened. Apparently, every Christmas she and her husband went home, their neighbour in the village would pick up sand, lift it to the heaven and decree that she will not live to see Sister Augustina have a child. This she did every Christmas for twenty-one years and Sister Augustina thought nothing of it. The Christmas she went home after the teaching, the same woman came to perform her ritual. Sister Augustina, picked up the earth as well and began to cancel the evil woman's words. She also decreed that the woman will not live to see her have a child, that means the woman will die because she must get pregnant. Three days after this encounter, the evil woman fell sick and was taken to hospital. Before the end of the week, she died. Three months later, Sister Augustina became pregnant and delivered.

- During a program in another of Jesus Sanctuary Ministries branch, people were asked to bring sand (Earth) from their compounds to pray with. After prayer, a young man who had collected the Earth from his father's compound, went back and spread the Earth back over the compound. Barely a week later, armed robbers came to their village, wreaking havoc in people's homes. As they got to his father's compound, they could not enter. Suddenly, the leader was heard clearly to say: "hurry up everyone, let us leave this place, the whole place is so hot, I can't keep my feet on the ground". That is how his father's compound was spared.

■ In another of Jesus Sanctuary Ministries branch, the Pastor said that the Earth would be used to pray against every satanic power fighting the church in the land. After prayers, the Pastor and the prayer warriors came back the next night to pray again. As they opened the Church, they saw a giant snake on the altar, stone dead. How the snake got into a locked church without any opening stunned every one.

■ Brother Colins is a member of one of Jesus Sanctuary Ministries branches. His desire was to attend one of the world renowned universities in England. He studied very hard and passed his examinations. After listening to teachings in the church about using the Earth to pray, he travelled to the university. Once on the university campus, he picked up the Earth and decreed that he must be admitted to that university. When the time for admission came, he was admitted to that university.

CHAPTER SIX

PRAYER POINTS

CONFESSION

Confession of sins is very important before going to God in prayers because sin can hinder our prayers from being answered. In Isaiah 59:1-2, the bible says:

"Behold, the Lord's hand is not shortened, that it cannot save; neither his ear heavy, that it cannot hear: But your iniquities have separated between you and your God, and your sins have hid his face from you, that he will not hear."

It is therefore imperative to confess every known and unknown sin as we come to God in prayers.

1

Romans 3:23

"For all have sinned, and come short of the glory of God"

O Lord my God, I confess all my sins and ask for your forgiveness and to cleanse me from all unrighteousness in Jesus Name, Amen.

2

Revelation 12:11

"And they overcame him by the blood of the Lamb, and by the word of their testimony; and they loved not their lives unto the death"

O Lord my God, I cover myself in the blood of Jesus Christ and I confess that the blood of Jesus Christ has rendered powerless Earthly strongholds in my life in Jesus' Name, Amen.

BINDING POWERS AND AUTHORITIES OF THE EARTH

God want us to prosper but some of us are not prospering because the evil ones are fighting against their blessings. Before our blessings can be released and come to us, we must first of all bind those evil powers hindering them. That is why Jesus said in Matthew 12:29:

"Or else how can one enter into a strong man's house, and spoil his goods, except he first bind the strong man? and then he will spoil his house."

The ability to bind and loose is a very powerful privilege of every child of God. In Matthew 18:18, Jesus said:

"Verily I say unto you, Whatsoever ye shall bind on earth shall be bound in heaven: and whatsoever ye shall loose on earth shall be loosed in heaven."

3

Matthew 18:18

"Verily I say unto you, Whatsoever ye shall bind on earth shall be bound in heaven: and whatsoever ye shall loose on earth shall be loosed in heaven"

O Lord my God, let the Earth and heaven bind whatsoever I have bound and loose whatsoever I have loosed in Jesus' Name, Amen.

4

Isaiah 60:2

"For, behold, the darkness shall cover the earth, and gross darkness the people: but the LORD shall arise upon thee, and his glory shall be seen upon thee"

O Lord my God, gross darkness will cover the secret enemies fighting me, in Jesus' Name, Amen.

5

1 Corinthians 8:5

"For though there be that are called gods, whether in heaven or in earth, (as there be gods many, and lords many)"

O Lord my God, I use the blood of Jesus to paralyse gods or lords controlling the land or property that I reside in, in Jesus' Name, Amen.

6

Job 20:27

"The heaven shall reveal his iniquity; and the earth shall rise up against him"

O Lord my God, all those paying evil for the good I have done, let the Earth rise up against them in Jesus' Name, Amen.

7

1 Samuel 28:13

"And the king said unto her, Be not afraid: for what sawest thou? And the woman said unto Saul, I saw gods ascending out of the earth"

O Lord my God, Earthly demons in my foundation, property, workplace, business place, place of worship and where I reside, assigned against me, be bound in Jesus' Name, Amen.

8

Jeremiah 10:11

"Thus shall ye say unto them, The gods that have not made the heavens and the earth, even they shall perish from the earth, and from under these heavens"

O Lord my God, I use the blood of Jesus to silence the voice or voices of gods speaking against my blessings and promotion in Jesus' Name, Amen.

9

Job 18:21

"Surely such are the dwellings of the wicked, and this is the place of him that knoweth not God"

O Lord my God, dwellings of the wicked, where they are calling my name for evil, be rendered desolate in Jesus' Name, Amen.

10

Leviticus 11:2

"Speak unto the children of Israel, saying, These are the beasts which ye shall eat among all the beasts that are on the earth"

O Lord my God, all the beasts of the Earth that are assigned to work against me, be rendered powerless in Jesus' Name, Amen.

11

Proverbs 2:22

"But the wicked shall be cut off from the earth, and the transgressors shall be rooted out of it"

O Lord my God, cut off and root out wicked ones assigned to hinder the blessings and favour of God upon my life, in Jesus' Name, Amen.

12 **Psalm 74:20**

"Have respect unto the covenant: for the dark places of the earth are full of the habitations of cruelty"

O Lord my God, whenever my name will be mentioned in the dark places of the Earth, the thunder of heaven will answer in Jesus' Name, Amen.

13 **Zephaniah 3:8**

"Therefore wait ye upon me, saith the LORD, until the day that I rise up to the prey: for my determination is to gather the nations, that I may assemble the kingdoms, to pour upon them mine indignation, even all my fierce anger: for all the earth shall be devoured with the fire of my jealousy"

O Lord my God, the Earth or land where people gather to plan against me, be devoured by fire in Jesus' Name, Amen.

14 **Isaiah 52:10**

"The LORD hath made bare his holy arm in the eyes of all the nations; and all the ends of the earth shall see the salvation of our God"

O Lord my God, all those fighting me without just cause, all the ends of the Earth will see their nakedness in Jesus' Name, Amen.

15

Jeremiah 27:5

"I have made the earth, the man and the beast that are upon the ground, by my great power and by my outstretched arm, and have given it unto whom it seemed meet unto me"

O Lord my God, the Earth, man and beast you have created will never hinder my blessings, promotions and favour of God and man in Jesus' Name, Amen.

16

Exodus 20:24

"An altar of earth thou shalt make unto me, and shalt sacrifice thereon thy burnt offerings, and thy peace offerings, thy sheep, and thine oxen: in all places where I record my name I will come unto thee, and I will bless thee"

O Lord my God, in any altar of Earth, where my pictures, clothing items, hair, nail, are used for evil divination and enchantment, I call forth the Fire of God upon those altars, in Jesus' Name, Amen.

17

Job 1:7

"And the LORD said unto Satan, Whence comest thou? Then Satan answered the LORD, and said, From going to and fro in the earth, and from walking up and down in it"

O Lord my God, the diviners and enchanters hired to fight me will continue to walk to and fro in the Earth until judgement comes upon them in Jesus' Name, Amen.

18 *Numbers 16:30*

"But if the LORD make a new thing, and the earth open her mouth, and swallow them up, with all that appertain unto them, and they go down quick into the pit; then ye shall understand that these men have provoked the LORD"

O Lord my God, as my sworn enemies gather to implement their wicked plan against me, let the Earth open her mouth and consume them in Jesus' Name, Amen.

19 *Genesis 9:13*

"I do set my bow in the cloud, and it shall be for a token of a covenant between me and the earth"

O Lord my God, I use the Blood of Jesus Christ to nullify satanic or demonic covenants between my foundation and the Earth in Jesus' Name, Amen.

20 *Joshua 7:9, Psalm 81:7*

"For the Canaanites and all the inhabitants of the land shall hear of it, and shall environ us round, and cut off our name from the earth: and what wilt thou do unto thy great name?" Psalms 81:7: "Thou calledst in trouble, and I delivered thee; I answered thee in the secret place of thunder: I proved thee at the waters of Meribah. Selah"

O Lord my God, those who want to cut off my name from the Earth, be answered in the secret place of thunder in Jesus' Name, Amen.

21

Genesis 6:20

"Of fowls after their kind, and of cattle after their kind, of every creeping thing of the earth after his kind, two of every sort shall come unto thee, to keep them alive"

O Lord my God, every creeping thing of the Earth, hindering my progress and blessing, be paralysed in Jesus' Name, Amen.

22

Revelation 7:1

"And after these things I saw four angels standing on the four corners of the earth, holding the four winds of the earth, that the wind should not blow on the earth, nor on the sea, nor on any tree"

O Lord my God, let the Angels that are in charge of the four corners of the Earth be in agreement and frustrate the wicked plans of the enemies after my blessings in Jesus' Name, Amen.

23

Lamentations 4:12

"The kings of the earth, and all the inhabitants of the world, would not have believed that the adversary and the enemy should have entered into the gates of Jerusalem"

O Lord my God, "kings" and "rulers" that are stumbling blocks to what God has ordained for me will never live to destroy me in Jesus' Name, Amen.

24 **Revelation 11:8**

"And their dead bodies shall lie in the street of the great city, which spiritually is called Sodom and Egypt, where also our Lord was crucified"

O Lord my God, all those who want to destroy my joy and happiness on the face of the Earth be destroyed by the Angels of God in Jesus' Name, Amen.

25 **Psalms 83:10**

"Which perished at Endor: they became as dung for the earth"

O Lord my God, let all those that hate me become as the waste of the Earth in Jesus' Name, Amen.

26 **Job 24:18**

"He is swift as the waters; their portion is cursed in the earth: he beholdeth not the way of the vineyards"

O Lord my God, all those imagining evil for me, their dwelling portion in the Earth be cursed forever in Jesus' Name, Amen.

27 **Genesis 4:14**

"Behold, thou hast driven me out this day from the face of the earth; and from thy face shall I be hid; and I shall be a fugitive and a vagabond in the earth; and it shall come to pass, that every one that findeth me shall slay me"

O Lord my God, from this day, drive from the face of the Earth all those that are incensed against me in Jesus' Name, Amen.

28

Job 38:24

"By what way is the light parted, which scattereth the east wind upon the earth?"

O Lord my God, in any place and time evil people will gather against me, let the east wind upon the Earth scatter them in Jesus' Name, Amen.

29

1 John 5:8

"And there are three that bear witness in earth, the Spirit, and the water, and the blood: and these three agree in one"

O Lord my God, let the three that bear witness in Earth (the spirit, the water, and the blood) witness in agreement against my sworn enemies, in Jesus' Name, Amen.

30

Jeremiah 28:16

"Therefore thus saith the LORD; Behold, I will cast thee from off the face of the earth: this year thou shalt die, because thou hast taught rebellion against the LORD"

O Lord my God, all those opposed to my well-being, cast them from the face of the Earth, in Jesus' Name, Amen.

31

Revelation 9:3

"And there came out of the smoke locusts upon the earth: and unto them was given power, as the scorpions of the earth have power"

O Lord my God, I use the powers in the Blood and Name of Jesus Christ, to tread upon on locusts and scorpions powers of the Earth, assigned against me in Jesus' Name, Amen.

32 **Genesis 6:4**

"There were giants in the earth in those days; and also after that, when the sons of God came in unto the daughters of men, and they bare children to them, the same became mighty men which were of old, men of renown"

O Lord my God, spiritual giants in the Earth assigned to hinder the glory and blessings of God upon my life be paralysed in Jesus' Name, Amen.

33 **Genesis 11:9**

"Therefore is the name of it called Babel; because the LORD did there confound the language of all the earth: and from thence did the LORD scatter them abroad upon the face of all the earth"

O Lord my God, all that hate me, confound their language and scatter them in Jesus' Name, Amen.

34 **Isaiah 24:18**

"And it shall come to pass, that he who fleeth from the noise of the fear shall fall into the pit; and he that cometh up out of the midst of the pit shall be taken in the snare: for the windows from on high are open, and the foundations of the earth do shake"

O Lord my God, let the foundation of the dwelling place of the wicked ones assigned against me, shake until they are consumed, in Jesus' Name, Amen.

35 | **Exodus 15:12**

"Thou stretchedst out thy right hand, the earth swallowed them"

O Lord my God, as the enemies will stretch out their evil hands against me, let the Earth swallow them in Jesus' Name, Amen.

36 | **Isaiah 54:12**

"And I will make thy windows of agates, and thy gates of carbuncles, and all thy borders of pleasant stones"

O Lord my God that made the Earth and created me upon it, You will never permit the strong man or women to bind me and spoil my blessings, promotion, favour and good name in Jesus' Name, Amen.

COMMANDING POWERS AND AUTHORITIES OF THE EARTH:

As we did mention, what govern the spirit realm are decrees and commands. The Earth, like any other creation of God, has the ability to obey commands and carry out instructions. All through the bible, God and even men of God, issued commands to the earth to do their will. In the same manner, we are to command the earth to obey us in order to accomplish our purposes. In Job 22:28, the bible says:

"Thou shalt also decree a thing, and it shall be established unto thee: and the light shall shine upon thy ways."

37

O earth, earth, earth, hear the word of the LORD. Thus saith the LORD, Write ye this man childless, a man that shall not prosper in his days: for no man of his seed shall prosper, sitting upon the throne of David, and ruling any more in Judah.

O Lord my God, O Earth, Earth, Earth, I decree and declare that you will never hear, understand or co-operate with the voice or voices of satanic or demonic ones or ones speaking against my expectations and blessings in Jesus' Name, Amen.

38

"And they sung as it were a new song before the throne, and before the four beasts, and the elders: and no man could learn that song but the hundred and forty and four thousand, which were redeemed from the earth"

O Lord my God, because the blood and Name of Jesus Christ has redeemed me from the Earth, I decree and declare that the ordinances (customs, laws, norms, rules) of the Earth should work in my favour in Jesus' Name, Amen.

39   **Psalms 67:6**

"Then shall the earth yield her increase; and God, even our own God, shall bless us"

O Lord my God, I decree and declare that the Earth yield her increase to me in Jesus' Name, Amen.

40   **Genesis 4:12**

"When thou tillest the ground, it shall not henceforth yield unto thee her strength; a fugitive and a vagabond shalt thou be in the earth"

O Lord my God, I decree and declare that I and my beloved ones will not be vagabonds in the Earth in Jesus' Name, Amen.

41   **Matthew 12:40**

"For as Jonas was three days and three nights in the whale's belly; so shall the Son of man be three days and three nights in the heart of the earth"

O Lord my God, I decree and declare that within three nights, my talents or blessings in the heart of the Earth be released in Jesus' Name, Amen.

42   **Psalms 41:2**

"The LORD will preserve him, and keep him alive; and he shall be blessed upon the earth: and thou wilt not deliver him unto the will of his enemies"

O Lord my God, I decree and declare that I and my seed will be blessed upon the Earth in Jesus' Name, Amen.

43 Genesis 8:22

"While the earth remaineth, seedtime and harvest, and cold and heat, and summer and winter, and day and night shall not cease"

O Lord my God, I decree and declare that while the Earth remains, seedtime and harvest will not cease in Jesus' Name, Amen.

44 Deuteronomy 28:1

"And it shall come to pass, if thou shalt hearken diligently unto the voice of the LORD thy God, to observe and to do all his commandments which I command thee this day, that the LORD thy God will set thee on high above all nations of the earth"

O Lord my God, I decree and declare from this day, the Lord God will set me on high above all the nations of the Earth in Jesus' Name, Amen.

45 Ecclesiastes 10:7

"I have seen servants upon horses, and princes walking as servants upon the earth"

O Lord my God, I decree and declare that I will never walk as a servant upon the Earth in Jesus' Name, Amen.

46 1 Kings 10:23

"So king Solomon exceeded all the kings of the earth for riches and for wisdom"

O Lord my God, I decree and declare that all the ends of the Earth will find me useful in Jesus' Name, Amen.

47 | **1 Samuel 26:20**

"Now therefore, let not my blood fall to the earth before the face of the LORD: for the king of Israel is come out to seek a flea, as when one doth hunt a partridge in the mountains"

O Lord my God, I decree and declare that my blood or hair will not fall to the Earth in Jesus' Name, Amen.

48 | **Job 38:4**

"Where wast thou when I laid the foundations of the earth? Declare, if thou hast understanding"

O Lord my God, I decree and declare that the foundation of the Earth laid by God, is speaking in my foundation in Jesus' Name, Amen.

49 | **Amos 3:5**

"Can a bird fall in a snare upon the Earth, where no gin is for him? Shall one take up a snare from the Earth and have taken nothing at all?"

O Lord my God, I decree and declare that snares or traps from the Earth aimed at me will never succeed in Jesus' Name, Amen.

50 | **Psalms 67:6**

"Then shall the earth yield her increase; and God, even our own God, shall bless us"

O Lord my God, I decree and declare that as long as I praise the Lord, the Earth will yield her increase to me in Jesus' Name, Amen.

51 Daniel 6:27

"He delivereth and rescueth, and he worketh signs and wonders in heaven and in earth, who hath delivered Daniel from the power of the lions"

O Lord my God, I decree and declare that the God that performs miracles in the Earth has delivered me from the power of the lions in Jesus' Name, Amen.

52 Proverbs 30:21

"For three things the earth is disquieted, and for four which it cannot bear"

O Lord my God, I decree and declare that the four things that disquiet or make the Earth uncomfortable will never be my portion in Jesus' Name, Amen.

53 Job 7:1

"Is there not an appointed time to man upon earth? Are not his days also like the days of an hireling?"

O Lord my God, I decree and declare that any satanic set time appointed for my failure, shame, scandal, sickness and death in the Earth has been nullified in Jesus' Name, Amen.

54 Psalms 11:3

"If the foundations be destroyed, what can the righteous do?"

O Lord my God, satanic foundations in my dwelling place or places be destroyed today in Jesus' Name, Amen.

55

Psalms 50:1

"The mighty God, even the LORD, hath spoken, and called the earth from the rising of the sun unto the going down thereof"

O Lord my God, I decree and declare that the Lord God that called the Earth from the rising of the sun unto the going down, will never allow the elemental forces to hinder the treasures of the Earth given to me in Jesus' Name, Amen.

56

Matthew 12:42

"The queen of the south shall rise up in the judgment with this generation, and shall condemn it: for she came from the uttermost parts of the earth to hear the wisdom of Solomon; and, behold, a greater than Solomon is here."

O Lord my God, I decree and declare that people from the uttermost parts of the Earth will be touched by the gifts and blessings of God upon my life in Jesus' Name, Amen.

57

Genesis 18:18

"Seeing that Abraham shall surely become a great and mighty nation, and all the nations of the earth shall be blessed in him?"

O Lord my God, I decree and declare that the nations and my generations will be blessed through me in Jesus' Name, Amen.

58

Matthew 6:10

"Thy kingdom come, Thy will be done in earth, as it is in heaven"

O Lord my God, I decree and declare that God's will established in heaven concerning my life must manifest on Earth in Jesus' Name, Amen.

59

Genesis 9:1

"And God blessed Noah and his sons, and said unto them, Be fruitful, and multiply, and replenish the earth"

O Lord my God, I decree and declare that I and my Seed will multiply and replenish the Earth in Jesus' Name, Amen.

60

Genesis 43:26

"And when Joseph came home, they brought him the present which was in their hand into the house, and bowed themselves to him to the earth"

O Lord my God, I decree and declare that household enemies in my life must bow themselves to me in Jesus' Name, Amen.

61

Matthew 5:13

"Ye are the salt of the earth: but if the salt have lost his savour, wherewith shall it be salted? it is thenceforth good for nothing, but to be cast out, and to be trodden under foot of men"

O Lord my God, I decree and declare that all the days of my life, I will ever be the salt of the Earth in Jesus' Name, Amen.

62

Job 22:28

"Thou shalt also decree a thing, and it shall be established unto thee: and the light shall shine upon thy ways"

My Father, My Father, I thank you for all what I commanded the Earth to hear and things decreed have been established, using the Name of Jesus Christ, Amen.

63

Matthew 12:29

"Or else how can one enter into a strong man's house, and spoil his goods, except he first bind the strong man? and then he will spoil his house"

O Lord my God, I bind and paralyse strong man or woman contending with God's plan and purpose for my life in Jesus' Name, Amen.

64

Numbers 23:23

"Surely there is no enchantment against Jacob, neither is there any divination against Israel: according to this time it shall be said of Jacob and of Israel, What hath God wrought!"

O Lord my God, I command the Earth to reject diviners' and enchanters' incantations against me in Jesus' Name, Amen.

65

Psalms 68:1

"Let God arise, let his enemies be scattered: let them also that hate him flee before him"

O Lord my God, as enemies gather on the face of the Earth against me, I command the Angels of God to scatter them in Jesus' Name, Amen.

66 **Genesis 4:10**

"And he said, What hast thou done? the voice of thy brother's blood crieth unto me from the ground"

O Lord my God, I use the Blood of Jesus Christ to nullify blood from the Earth crying or speaking against God's plan and purpose for my life in Jesus' Name, Amen.

67 **Psalms 74:20**

"Have respect unto the covenant: for the dark places of the earth are full of the habitations of cruelty"

O Lord my God, dark places of the Earth where my names are being invoked for affliction, I command the fire of heaven to consume such places in Jesus' Name, Amen.

68 **Psalms 49:15**

"But God will redeem my soul from the power of the grave: for he shall receive me. Selah"

O Lord my God, anyone that will ever use the power of the Earth (grave) to fight me, I command demons of the Earth to turn against them in Jesus' Name, Amen.

69 **Jeremiah 1:13**

"And the word of the LORD came unto me the second time, saying, What seest thou? And I said, I see a seething pot; and the face thereof is toward the north"

O Lord my God, satanic or demonic pots buried in the Earth in order to fight or contend with my promotion, be destroyed in Jesus' Name, Amen.

70

Isaiah 54:15

"Behold, they shall surely gather together, but not by me: whosoever shall gather together against thee shall fall for thy sake"

O Lord my God, whenever evil people will gather against me on the face of the Earth, I command the Earth to rise up against them in Jesus' Name, Amen.

71

Colossians 2:14

"Blotting out the handwriting of ordinances that was against us, which was contrary to us, and took it out of the way, nailing it to his cross"

O Lord my God, I use the Blood of Jesus Christ, to blot out handwriting of ordinances that has been written against me in my dwelling place, in Jesus' Name, Amen.

72

Mark 6:11

"And whosoever shall not receive you, nor hear you, when ye depart thence, shake off the dust under your feet for a testimony against them. Verily I say unto you, It shall be more tolerable for Sodom and Gomorrha in the day of judgment, than for that city"

O Lord my God, anyone paying me evil in return for the good done to him or her, let the dust of the Earth witness against the person in Jesus' Name, Amen.

73

Exodus 8:16

"And the LORD said unto Moses, Say unto Aaron, Stretch out thy rod, and smite the dust of the land, that it may become lice throughout all the land of Egypt"

O Lord my God, secret enemies in my life, let the dust of the Earth's afflictions be their portion in Jesus' Name, Amen.

74

Genesis 13:8

"And Abram said unto Lot, Let there be no strife, I pray thee, between me and thee, and between my herdmen and thy herdmen; for we be brethren"

O Lord my God, the Earth will not allow household enemies to perform their evil plans against me in Jesus' Name, Amen.

75

Isaiah 26:21

"For, behold, the LORD cometh out of his place to punish the inhabitants of the earth for their iniquity: the earth also shall disclose her blood, and shall no more cover her slain"

O Lord my God, I decree and declare that the Earth will disclose, expose and reject satanic blood sacrifices crying against my breakthrough in Jesus' Name, Amen.

76

Isaiah 54:17

"No weapon that is formed against thee shall prosper; and every tongue that shall rise against thee in judgment thou shalt condemn. This is the heritage of the servants of the LORD, and their righteousness is of me, saith the LORD"

O Lord my God, I command satanic arrows from the graveyards, T-Junctions, market place, roundabout and evil lands, to return back to their senders in Jesus' Name, Amen.

77

Psalms 121:6

"The sun shall not smite thee by day, nor the moon by night"

O Lord my God, any man or woman that will ever pick up the Earth and speak to the sun, moon and stars for evil, will receive the judgement of the elemental forces in Jesus' Name, Amen.

78

Psalms 89:51

"Wherewith thine enemies have reproached, O LORD; wherewith they have reproached the footsteps of thine anointed"

O Lord my God, all those that will or have collected my foot-prints or car-prints for evil, will not live to carry out their plans in Jesus' Name, Amen.

Thank God for answered prayers.

NOTES

NOTES

NOTES